BIG·BOOK·OF
A B C

Illustrated by David Anstey

GALLERY BOOKS
An Imprint of W. H. Smith Publishers Inc.
112 Madison Avenue
New York City 10016

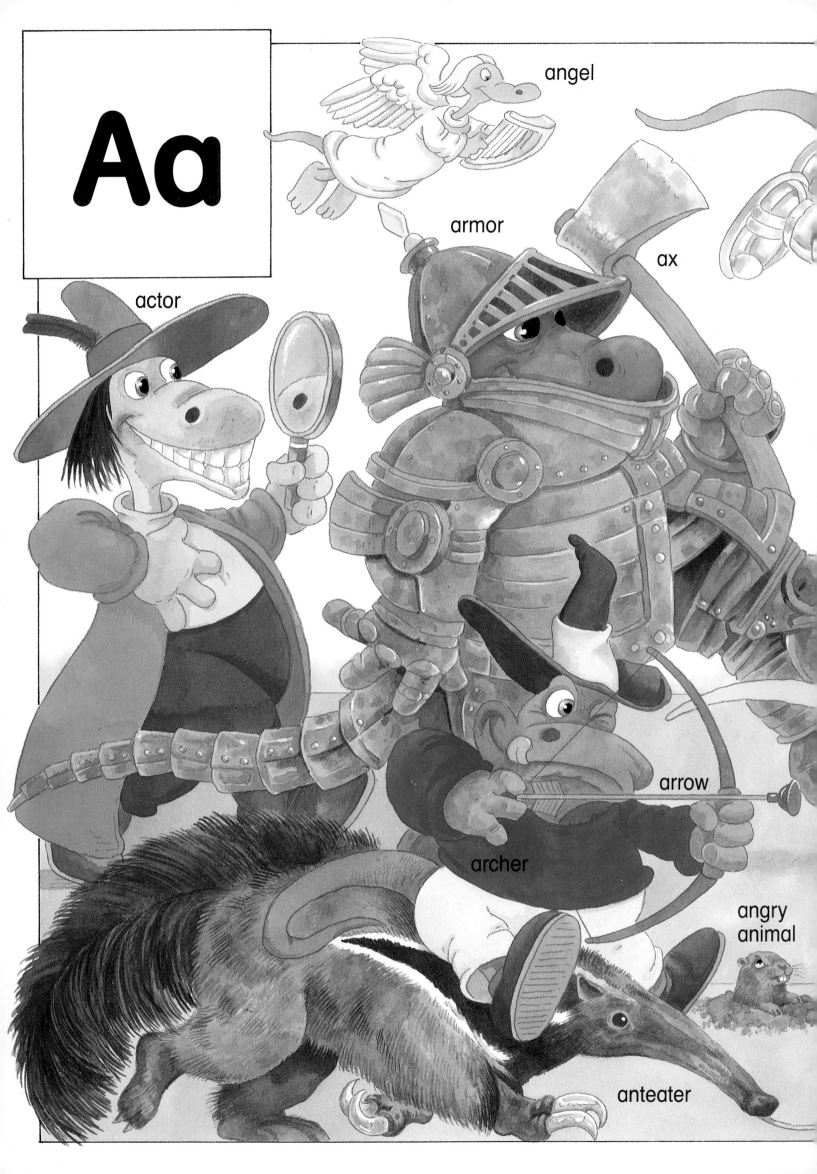

astronaut

airplane

Aunt Alice is an athlete

anchor

anorak

arm

ace

apron

ankle

apple

acorn

armadillo

artist

alarmed
ant

another
ant

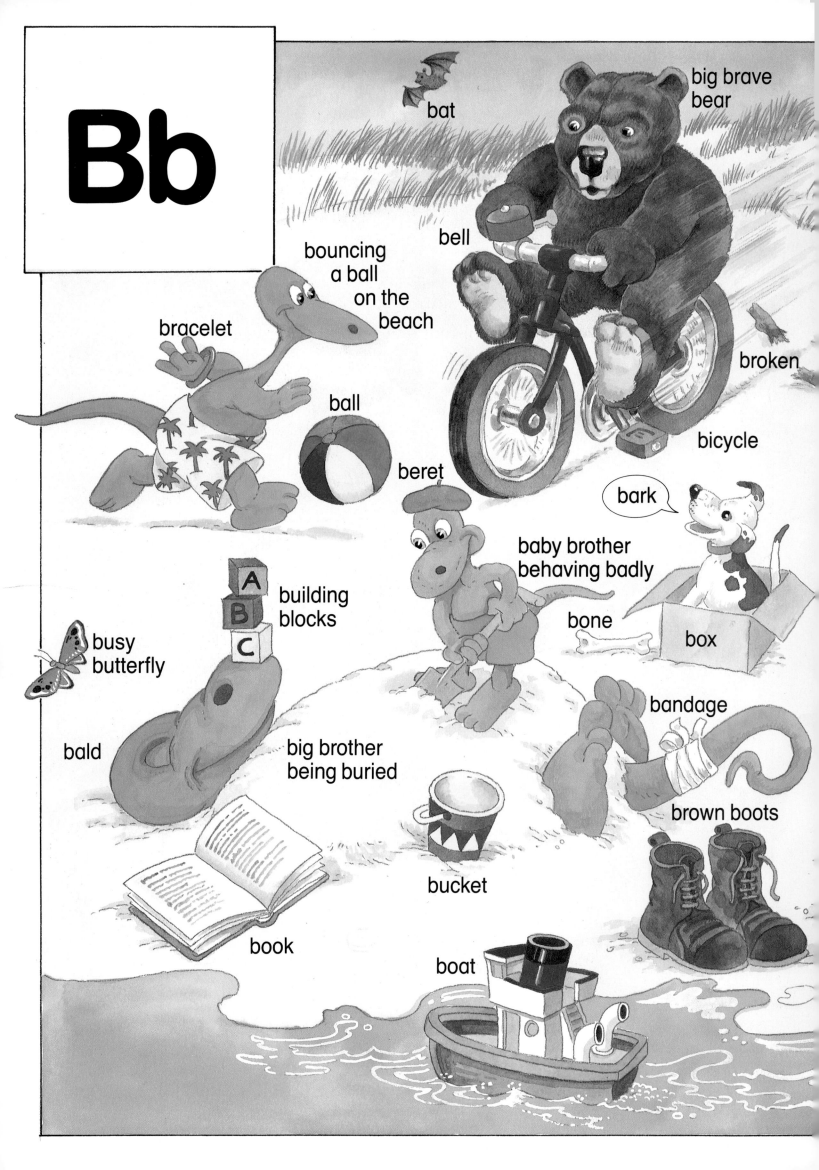

bush with berries

big black bird

bee

beak

bread and butter

bottle

beans

bowl

bow tie

beautiful beads

bikini

blue blanket

bag

banana

beetle

balloon

bird watching

braces

bird balancing on a boulder

belt

bright buttons

Cc

clock
coconut
china cup
crack
cat
comb
cry
chocolate
chin
curious crocodile
curl
children
clever cowboy climbing carefully up the cupboard
camel
car
collar
can
celery
cow
cake covered with candles
cabbage
castle
cauliflower
cheerful clown in a colorful coat
curtains
carrot
caterpillar

daddy

daughter

drawings

desert

Dinah is a dainty dancer

Dd

doctor

desk

door

drive

duck

dinosaur

dog

dove

dangerous dragon

dolphin

deer

donkey

drumstick

daffodil

dandelion

doll

drum

doughnut

dress

dreaming

dish

Hh

Ii

important
indian
eating
ice cream

interesting
insect

iceberg

iron

ironing
board

ivy

ill

island

ink

Jj

jam
jar

jewel

jumping

jolly juggler
in the
jungle

jigsaw

jet

jacket

jersey

jeans

jogging

Kk

the king knows a
knight who wears
a kilt

key

kettle

kite

kitten

knot

kennel

knives

kilt

kick

kangaroo

kneeling

knee

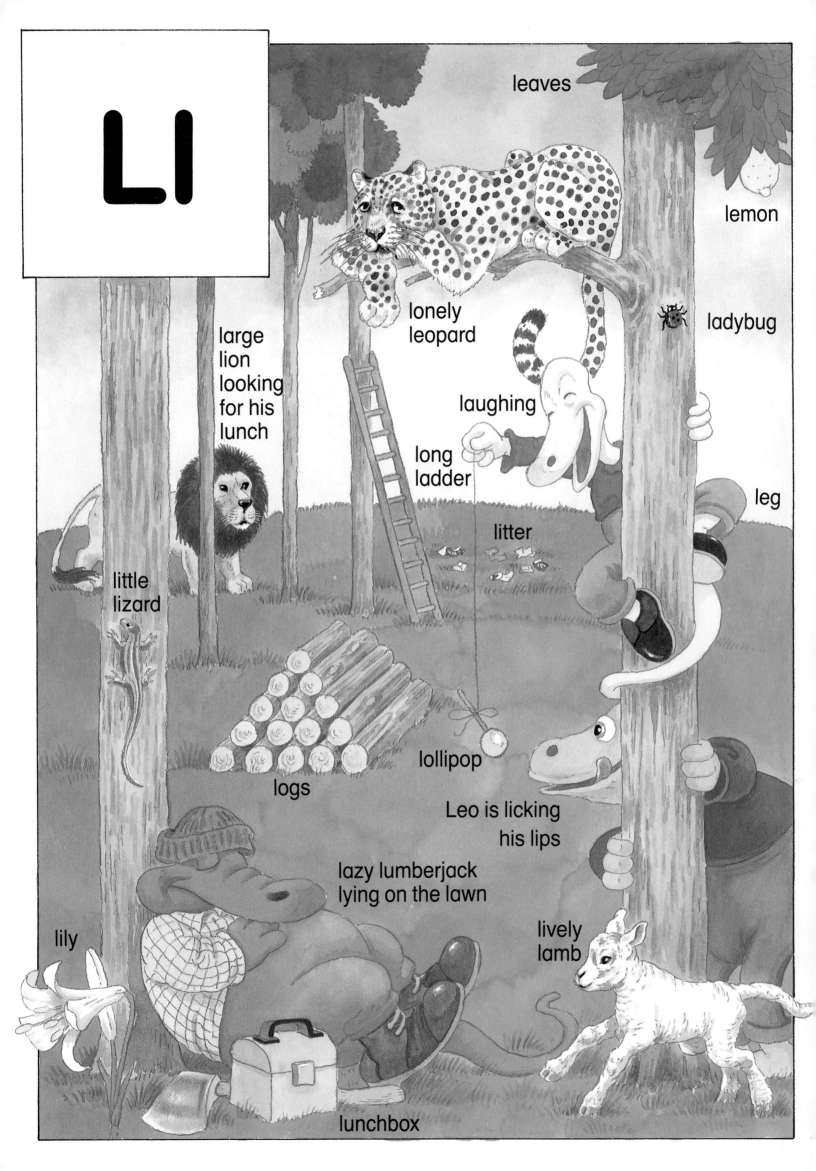

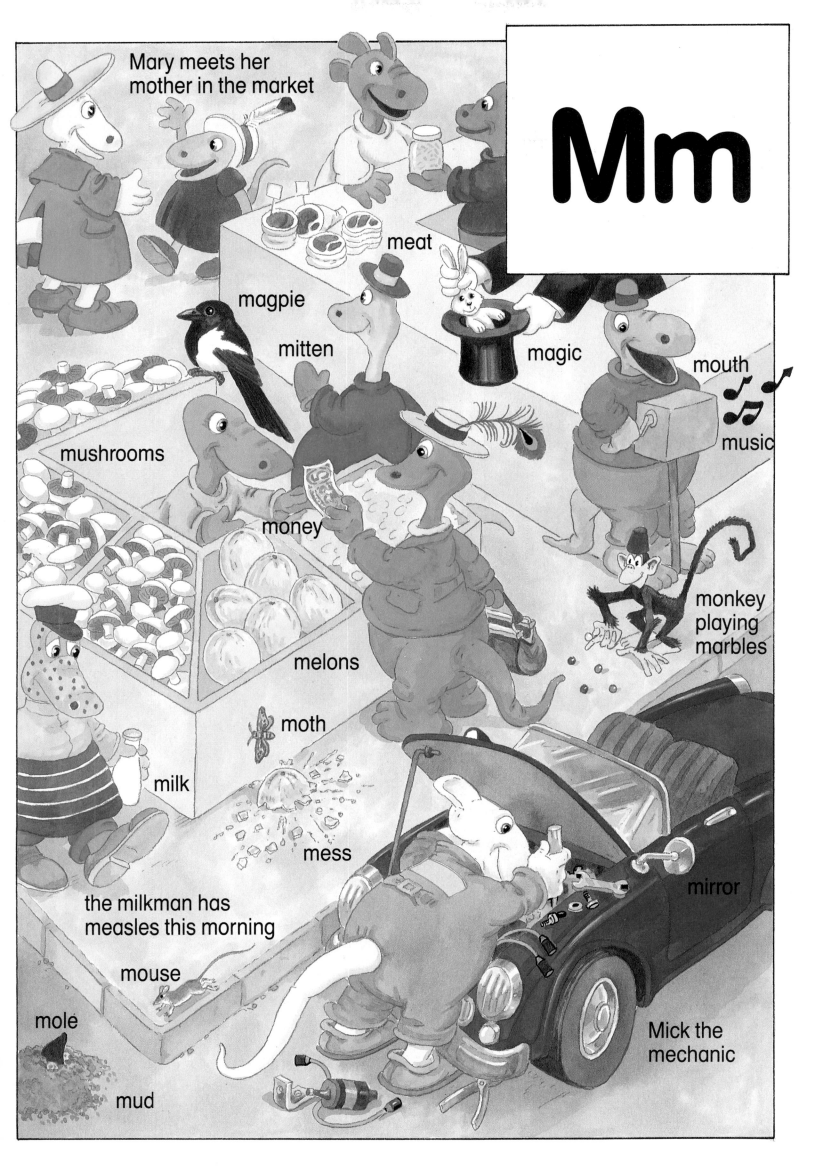

Mary meets her mother in the market

Mm

meat

magpie

mitten

magic

mouth

music

mushrooms

money

melons

monkey playing marbles

moth

milk

mess

mirror

the milkman has measles this morning

mouse

mole

Mick the mechanic

mud

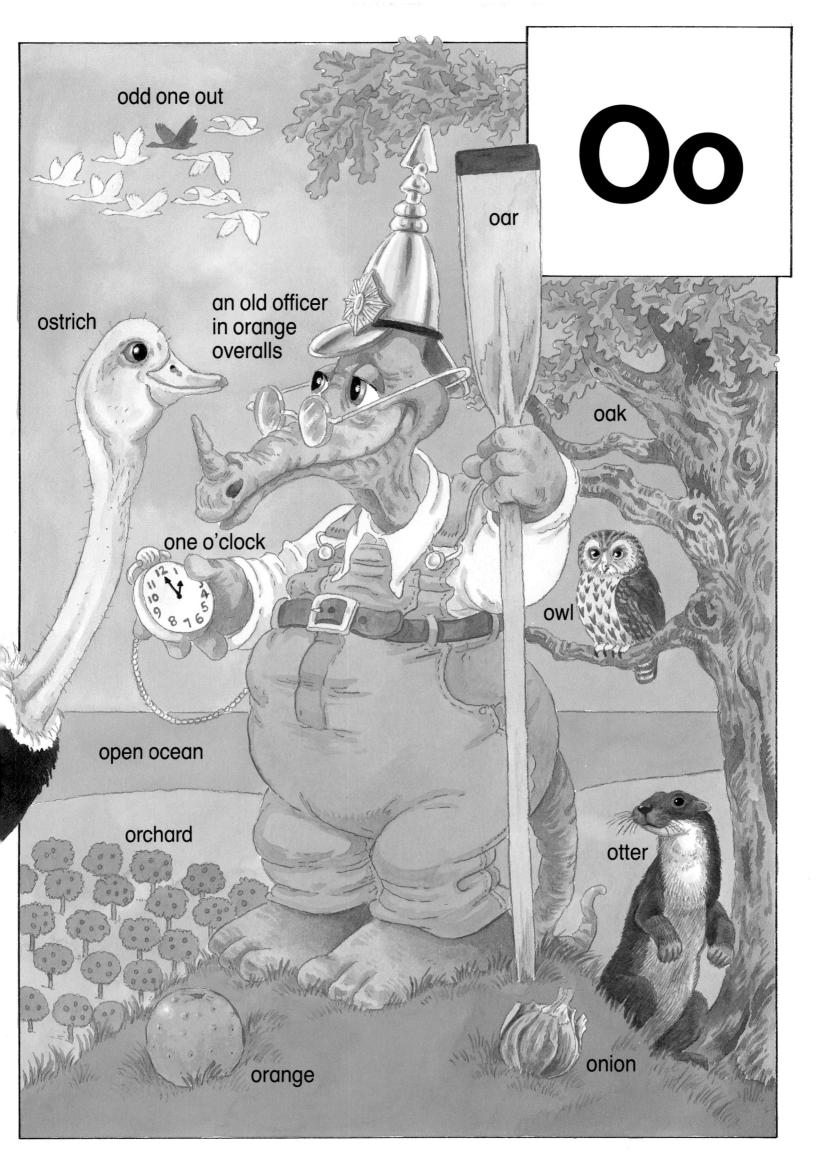

Pp

Plum's party

polar bear

playing party games

prisoner

Plum

a pair of pigeons

pretty pink dress

patting the pet poodle

a perching parrot

penguin

patch

pocket

pizza

pears

puppet

pirate

paint

photographer

Poppy putting on a paper hat

painting pretty patterns

Qq

quietly viewing the queen's quads

queen

quarrel

quilt

quack

quail

rain

a robot riding a reindeer

river

reporter

raincoat

row of rhubarb

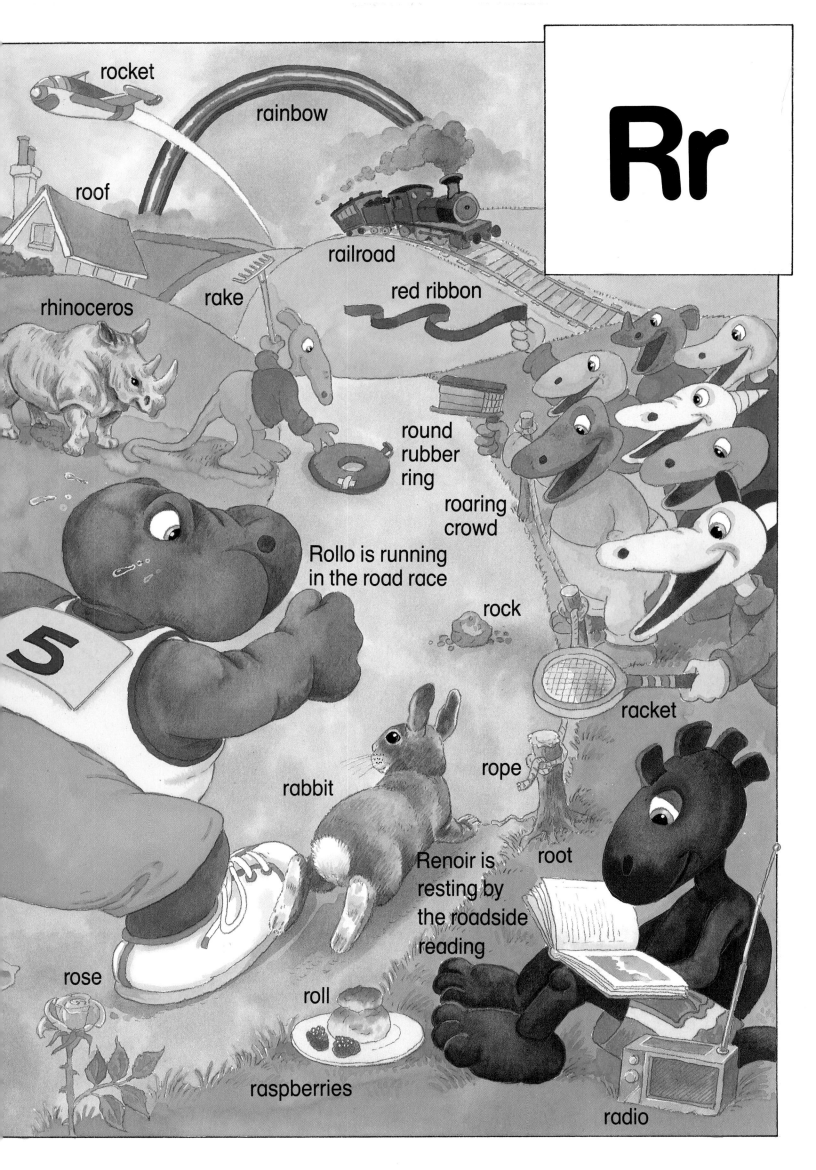

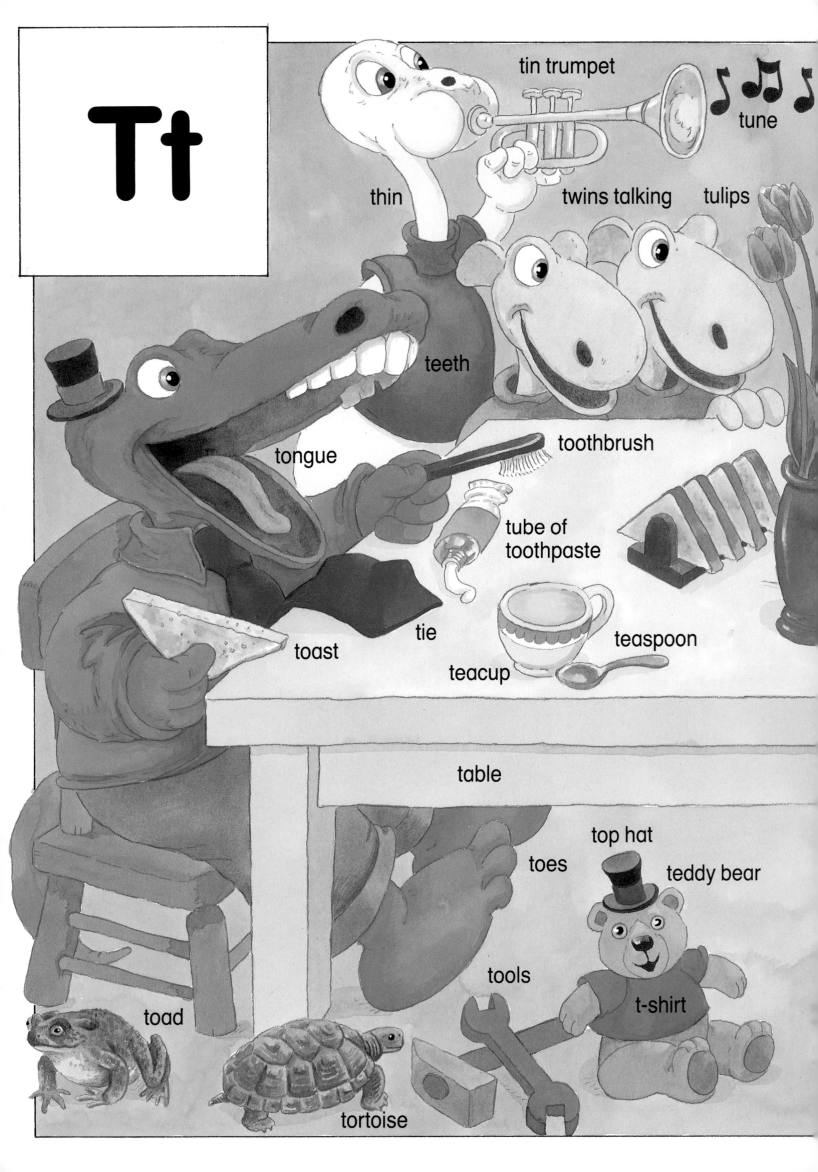

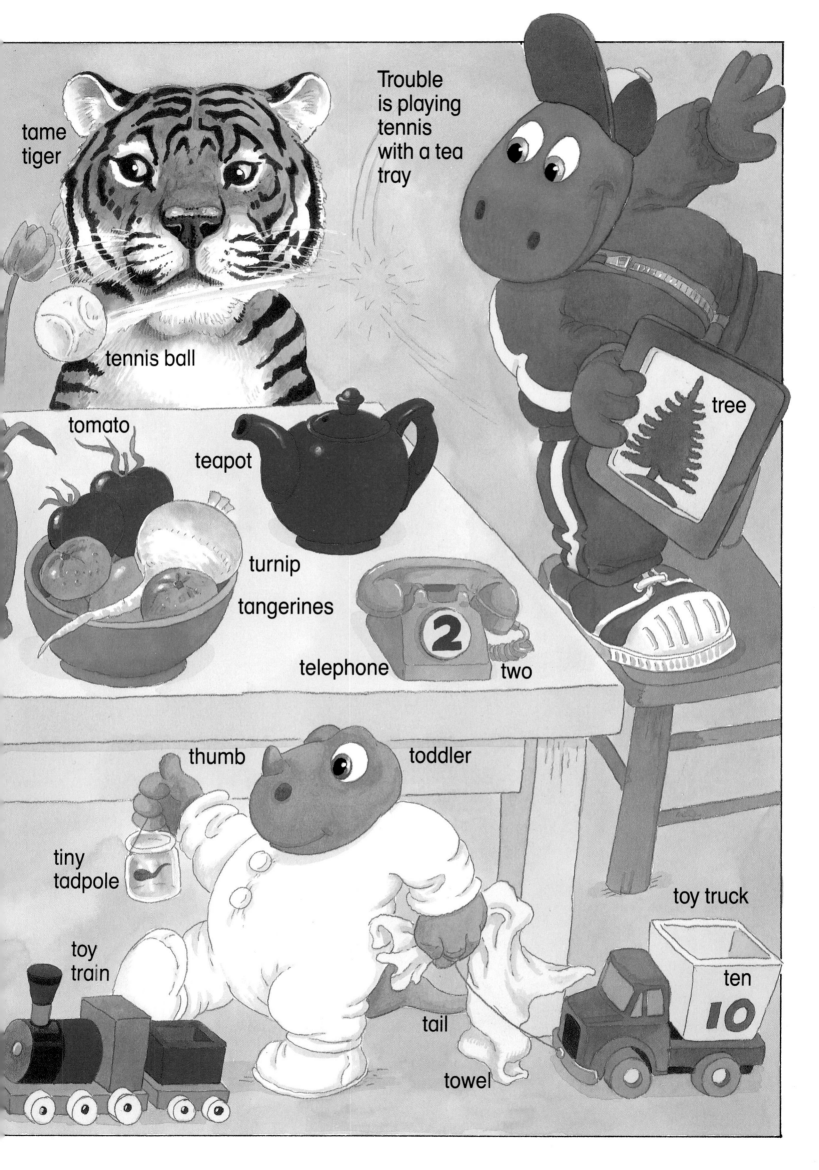

tame tiger

tennis ball

Trouble is playing tennis with a tea tray

tree

tomato

teapot

turnip

tangerines

telephone

two

thumb

toddler

tiny tadpole

toy truck

toy train

tail

ten

towel

Uu

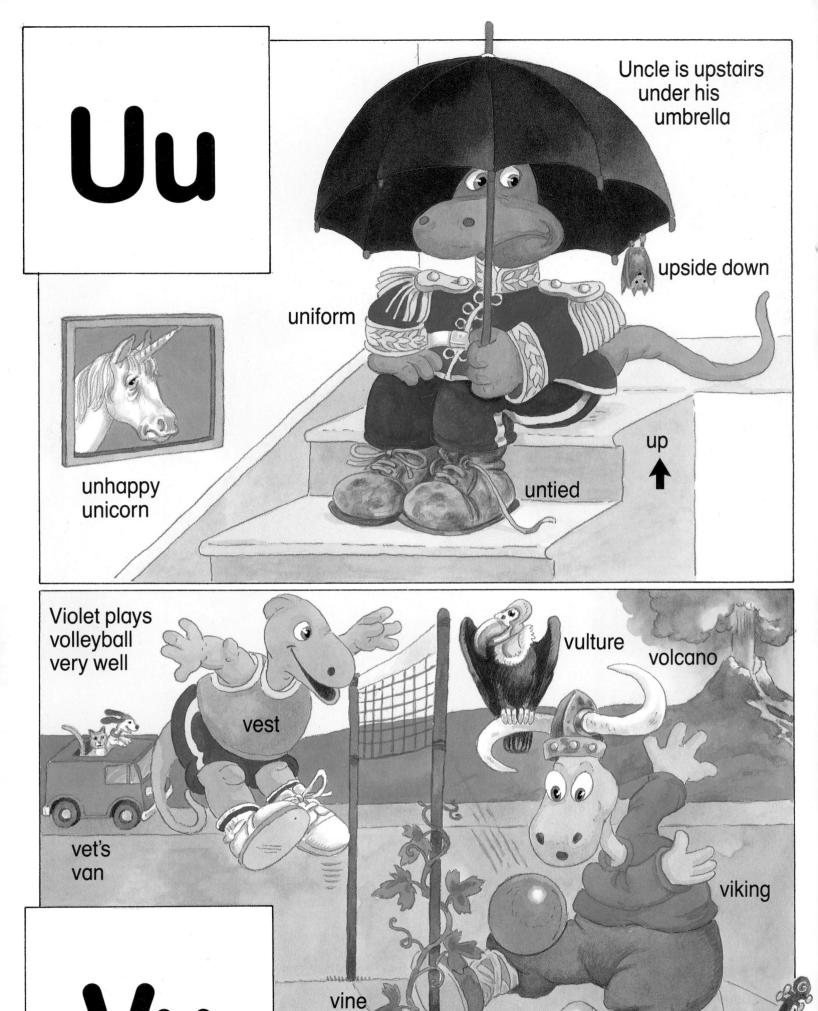

Uncle is upstairs under his umbrella

upside down

uniform

up

untied

unhappy unicorn

Vv

Violet plays volleyball very well

vulture

volcano

vest

vet's van

viking

vine

violet

valuable violin

witch waving

web

window

wall

Waldo whistles
as he walks
by the water
in winter

wood

white

wild
wolf

wheel

whiskers

warm wool
vest

wristwatch

worried
worm

weed

water

Ww

Xx

x-ray

xylophone

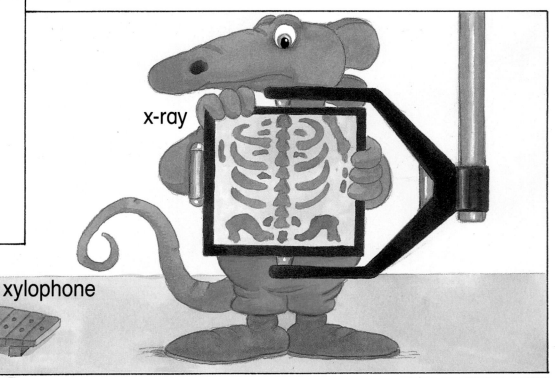

Yy

yawn

yo-yo

young yak

yellow yacht

Zz

seeing zebras at the zoo

zebra

ZOO

zig-zag

zipper